D1222609

STAGE SCHOOL

BALLET DANCER

LISA REGAN

WINDMILL
BOOKS
New York

Published in 2013 by Windmill Books, An Imprint of Rosen Publishing
29 East 21st Street, New York, NY 10010

Produced for Windmill by Calcium Creative Ltd
Editors for Calcium Creative Ltd: Sarah Eason and Vicky Egan
US Editor: Sara Antill
Designer: Nick Leggett

Cover: Dreamstime: Sinan Isakovic fg; Shutterstock: Aida Ricciardiello bg.
Inside: Dreamstime: Pavel Losevsky 13, Jack Q 22; Shutterstock: Yuri Arcurs
10, Samuel Borges 5, Igor Bulgarin 15, 23, Carlush 6, Carlo Dapino 11, Df028
24, Jaimie Duplass 17, Pavel Ganchev 3, Holbox 27, Nataliya Hora 20, Sinan
Isakovic 28, J Hersh Photo 8, 12, Gordan Milic 26, Sean Nel 7, Alias Studiot
Oy 21, Sergey Petrov 4, 9, Picamaniac 1, Jack Q 14, 16, 18, 19, 29,
Maksym Vlasenko 25.

Library of Congress Cataloging-in-Publication Data

Regan, Lisa, 1971–
  Ballet dancer / by Lisa Regan.
     p. cm. — (Stage school)
Includes index.
  ISBN 978-1-4488-8091-1 (library binding) — ISBN 978-1-4488-8150-5 (pbk.)
  — ISBN 978-1-4488-8156-7 (6-pack)
1. Ballet dancing—Juvenile literature. 2. Ballet dancers—Juvenile literature.
I. Title.
  GV1787.5.R43 2013
  792.802'8092—dc23
                          2012005288

Manufactured in the United States of America

CPSIA Compliance Information: Batch #B3S12WM: For Further Information contact Windmill Books, New York, New York at 1-866-478-0556

CONTENTS

BALLET IS BEAUTIFUL!

Watching a ballet is magical. It takes you to another world of make-believe, beautiful costumes, and wonderful stories. The dancers in a ballet use music and dance to tell a story.

Princesses and witches

Many ballets feature princesses and heroes, good and bad **fairies**, and wicked witches, too. Many ballet stories are based on fairy tales that were written a long time ago.

⬇ *Ballet dancers are as strong and fit as athletes.*

Learning to dance

Imagine what it must be like to be in a ballet yourself! Attending ballet classes is a lot of fun. You will become strong and fit, learn to move and balance with grace and skill, and make new friends, too! What are you waiting for?

⇩ *If you join a ballet class when you are young, you may find you have a hobby for life!*

WHAT TO WEAR

All ballet dancers wear the same type of clothes. The clothes stretch easily and are comfortable to dance in. They also fit tightly to the body so that the dance teacher can see all of the dancer's movements.

Made for dancing

Ballet shoes are made of soft leather or satin. They are held on to the dancer's foot with elastic or ribbon. Dancers clean their shoes carefully before a performance so that they look perfect on stage.

⇨ *Ballet shoes are usually pink, cream, or white. Sometimes the sole is split (see the photograph on page 5) so that the foot can bend more easily.*

For the girls

Girls should wear their hair in a neat style so that it does not cover their faces. It can be tied back into a bun or braided. Girls with short hair can pull it back with an elastic headband.

For the boys

Male ballet dancers usually wear their hair short, or tied back with a band if they have long hair.

BE A STAR

You will need:

- For girls: Leotard and tights
- For boys: T-shirt and stretchy shorts or tights
- Ballet shoes
- Shoe bag (to keep your shoes neat and clean)
- Bottle of water
- Extras: Wraparound cardigan, **leg warmers**, skirt

⇧ *Male ballet dancers wear tight clothes that stretch easily and ballet shoes.*

7

IN TRAINING

Your ballet teacher will teach you new **positions**, which will make you stretch your body. You'll need to lift your legs higher than normal, and bend your body lower. Ballet improves your muscle strength and your **posture**.

Turned out toes

If you watch a ballet dancer walking, you might think he or she waddles like a duck! This is because dancers train their feet and legs to turn outward, so that their toes point away from each other.

▷ *Practice turning your legs and hips outward. At the same time, hold your arms above your head.*

IN THE SPOTLIGHT

Getting in shape
A scientific study has found that **professional** ballet dancers are often in better shape than Olympic swimmers!

A hard workout

Adult ballet dancers practice for hours and hours to improve their skills and increase their strength so that they can perform lifts.

Performing lifts

A male dancer must be strong enough to lift his partner, and the female dancer must have strong muscles so that she can hold herself in the correct position.

⇨ *Professional dancers can move their bodies into amazing positions!*

TURNING OUT

Young ballet dancers are taught to hold their legs, feet, arms, and hands in five basic positions. These help the dancers to balance as they dance, and also make their movements look graceful. In all ballets, the movements start and end in one of the five positions.

➡ *Ballet positions help dancers to create beautiful shapes as they perform.*

Second, third, and fourth position

To change from first position to second, raise your arms halfway, move them apart, and slide one foot away from the other. In third position, the heel of the front foot touches the middle of the back foot. To change to fourth position, slide the front foot forward a little, keeping the toes turned outward.

There are various positions for the arms in third and fourth position, depending on which **method** of ballet you learn.

⇨ *In fifth position, the arms curve gracefully above the head and the feet turn outward with the toes touching the heels.*

BALLET CLASS

Ballet classes will teach you how important it is to hold your body properly. One wall of a dance studio is lined with huge mirrors, so that you can watch yourself and see which position you are in as you dance during class.

⇦ *When you perform a ballet movement, check your body position in the mirror.*

BE A STAR

Dancing at home
You can practice ballet at home. Wear your ballet clothes, and always warm up. Use the edge of a table to help you to balance, but be sure that there is plenty of space all around you.

Barre work

Much of the ballet lesson will be spent at the barre (a long handrail). Usually the barre is attached to the wall in front of the mirrors. The exercises you do at the barre will warm up your muscles and improve your balance and footwork.

On the floor

Some of the time in a ballet class will be spent doing floor work in the center of the room. There you will link steps together, sometimes with leaps and turns.

⇩ *The ballet teacher checks that each dancer at the barre is performing her moves correctly.*

BALLET MUSIC

Ballet practice is done to music played either on a CD or on a piano in the studio. The piano player stops playing whenever the teacher wants to talk to his or her students. The piano player can replay a piece of music if the teacher wants the dancers to repeat their movements.

⬇ *The music from* **Swan Lake** *is full of action and surprises.*

Writing ballet music

The music for a ballet performance is written by a **composer** and is called a score. The music must have a strong rhythm so that the dancers can step in time to the beat.

Storytelling music

Ballet music often helps to tell the story. The music slows down when something sad happens in the story. The music speeds up when something exciting happens in the ballet.

⬇ **The Nutcracker** *has lively, fun music that tells the story of magical toys.*

CHOREOGRAPHY

The person who plans the steps in a ballet is called the choreographer. He or she may work with a composer to create a new ballet, or may listen to the music of an old ballet and make up new movements to go with it.

Making changes

Once a choreographer has planned all the steps, he or she works with the dancers to get the moves just right. The choreographer may keep changing the steps to make the ballet look better.

⬇ *A good dancer must remember her moves and quickly learn any changes that the choreographer makes.*

⇨ *You can be your own choreographer! Watch yourself in the mirror and make up your dance moves.*

Keeping notes

Did you know that a dance can be written down? A choreologist writes down every move in a ballet. The record that he or she makes is called **notation**. It has small markings on a set of five lines, and looks similar to written music.

OUT ON YOUR OWN

When a ballet dancer joins a ballet **company**, she starts by dancing with other dancers in a group called the corps de ballet. As she improves she may be chosen to dance on her own, as a soloist, in front of the group.

⇩ *Every dancer in the corps de ballet may wear the same costume so that they appear as a group.*

Moving together

The corps de ballet dancers often have to make exactly the same moves at the same time. If one person makes a mistake, it will show!

Taking the lead

A ballet dancer who is good enough to dance the lead part in a ballet is called the **principal dancer**. A principal dancer often travels the world and dances with different ballet companies.

➡️ *The principal female dancer is sometimes called the prima ballerina.*

BE A STAR

Find a partner
Ask a ballet friend to be your dance partner so that you can practice moves together. A dance for two people is called a pas de deux or a duet.

19

CHANGING STYLES

Ballet began over 400 years ago. At that time, all the dancers were men, and the ballets had no storyline. In the 1800s **Romantic ballets**, such as *Giselle* and *La Sylphide*, became popular. They included characters such as **spirits**, fairies, and witches.

⬇ *In the ballet* Giselle, *the heroine dies of a broken heart.*

When dancing en pointe, a ballet dancer must arch her foot to avoid injury.

On tiptoes

Romantic ballet introduced the idea of dancing on tiptoes, known as dancing en pointe. It was made famous in the 1820s by Marie Taglioni (1804–1884). Ballerinas en pointe appear to float above the stage.

Time for change

At the end of the 1800s ballet changed again. **Classical ballets**, such as *Swan Lake* and *The Sleeping Beauty*, lasted for hours. These long ballets allowed ballerinas to show off dance moves, jumps, and lifts that required skill and strength.

IN THE SPOTLIGHT

Magical movements

George Balanchine (1904–1983) was a Russian choreographer who moved away from classical ballet. For him, creating beautiful dance movements was more important than telling a story.

TELLING A STORY

A ballet performance is made up of more than just the dancers' steps. While the dancers' movements are very important, costumes, makeup, lighting, and set design also play a big part in creating a wonderful ballet.

Different styles

Many ballets tell well-known stories, such as fairy tales. Others tell less well-known stories, or just create different moods. The music and costumes help to show which characters are important, which are good or bad, and whether something **dramatic** is happening.

➡ *The principal dancers in a ballet wear dramatic costumes so that they stand out from the corps de ballet.*

Look them up!
Find out all you can about famous ballet stories such as *Swan Lake* and *The Nutcracker*.

⇩ *Red lights are used to create an exciting mood.*

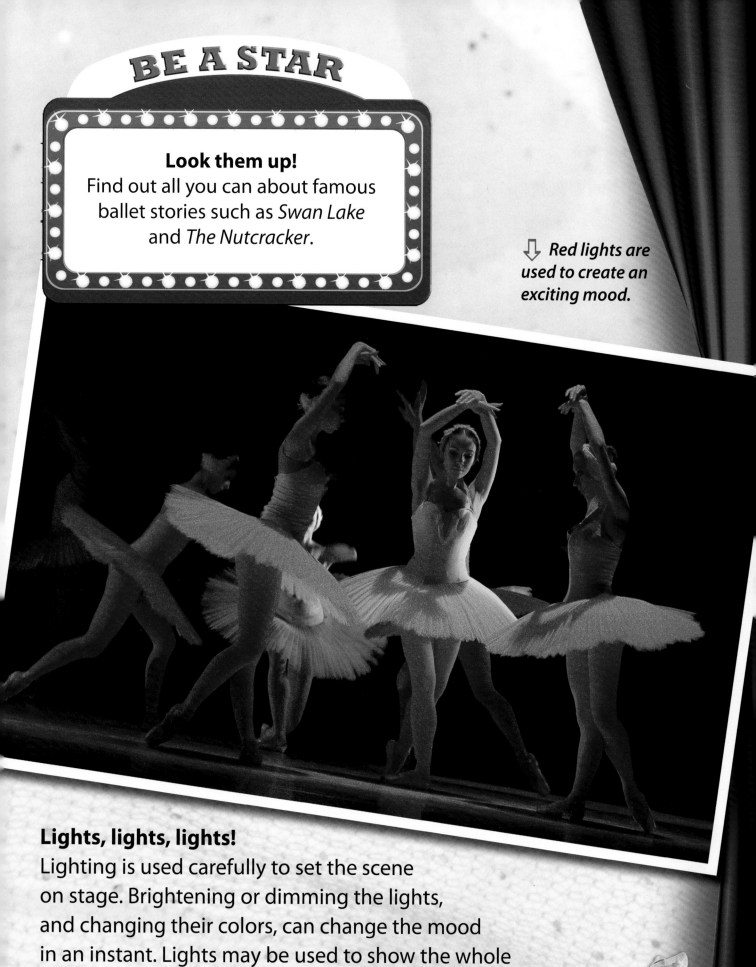

Lights, lights, lights!
Lighting is used carefully to set the scene on stage. Brightening or dimming the lights, and changing their colors, can change the mood in an instant. Lights may be used to show the whole stage, or just to pick out the principal dancers.

While the choreographer decides the dance steps for the ballet, the designers plan what the stage will look like.

Set design

The stage is often decorated with a painted backdrop that shows where the ballet is taking place. It might show a town, a forest, or an indoor scene, such as a child's bedroom or a palace.

⬇ *Some ballets have an almost empty stage. Others use real furniture.*

Beatrix Potter
The dancers in the *Tales of Beatrix Potter* ballet have to perform amazing leaps and turns while wearing animal costumes and masks!

⇦ *Black costumes are often worn to show that a character is evil.*

Costumes
In classical ballet, ballerinas often wear a short, ruffled skirt called a tutu. This shows off a dancer's body, and lets people see the beautiful shapes she makes as she moves. Important characters, such as the evil fairy Carabosse in *The Sleeping Beauty* or the mysterious Drosselmeyer in *The Nutcracker*, wear very dramatic costumes.

GOING TO THE BALLET

Attending your very first ballet performance should be a magical experience that you remember forever. The excitement begins even before the curtain rises.

Tuning up

The music is played by an **orchestra**. The musicians sit out of sight of the audience in the orchestra pit, which is a sunken area between the stage and the front row of seats. Before the show starts, you will hear the musicians tuning their instruments.

⬇ *In many classical and Romantic ballets, a full orchestra plays the music.*

So much to see

At the start of a ballet, the
lights go dim and the curtain
rises. You will soon forget
everything around you as you
watch the dancers making their
beautiful shapes. At the end of the
performance, the audience may stand
to clap if they think the ballerinas
have danced particularly well.

*⇦ Don't forget
to take a bow at
the end of your
own magical
performance!*

BALLET TALK

When King Louis XIV of France set up his royal ballet, he named the ballet steps. Many of those French words are still used today. If you want to be a ballet dancer, you'll have to learn some new words as well as steps!

⇐ *When you practice a ballet move, try to remember its name.*

BE A STAR

Get the lingo!
If you learn as many of the ballet terms as you can now, you will find it much easier to follow the teacher's instructions when she teaches you a new dance.

FRENCH BALLET TERMS

Try to learn one new ballet term every week. Here are just a few that you can practice:

arabesque (a-ruh-BESK)
Standing on one leg with the other leg lifted behind, with the foot pointed.

battement (bat-MOHN)
A beating movement or kick with a straight leg.

chassé (sha-SAY)
A "chasing" step repeated quickly.

demi-plié (DEH-mee-plee-ay)
Bending the knees halfway, while keeping the heels firmly on the ground.

fouetté (fweh-TAY)
A sharp, fast, "whipping" movement.

jeté (zheh-TAY)
A jump from one foot to the other.

pirouette (peer-uh-WET)
A spin of the whole body on one foot.

plié (plee-AY)
Bending at the knee while the back is held straight.

⇨ *Great skill and strength are needed to perform an arabesque.*

GLOSSARY

classical ballets
(KLA-sih-kul BA-lays)
Ballets that tell a story,
usually in sections (acts).

company (KUMP-nee)
A group of dancers who
perform together.

composer (kom-POH-zer)
Someone who writes music.

dramatic (druh-MAT-ik)
Striking, powerful, effective.

fairies (FAYR-eez)
Human-shaped creatures with
magical powers. They often cause
trouble in a playful way.

leg warmers (LEHG WORM-erz)
Footless long socks that dancers
wear to keep their leg muscles
warm and relaxed.

method (MEH-thud)
A way of doing something. Ballet
schools in different countries use
different methods to teach ballet.

notation (noh-TAY-shun)
Dance moves that are
written down.

orchestra (OR-kes-truh)
A large group of musicians that
perform together on string, wind,
brass, and percussion instruments.

positions (puh-ZIH-shunz)
One of five different ways to place
the arms and feet, with the legs
turned out at the hips.

posture (PAHS-chur)
The way in which a person
stands and holds their body.

principal dancer
(PRIN-sih-pul DAN-ser)
The leading male or female dancer
in a ballet company.

professional (pruh-FESH-nul)
Someone who is paid to do a task.

Romantic ballets
(roh-MAN-tik BA-lays)
Ballets written between about 1827
and 1870. Some Romantic ballets
feature spirits or ghosts.

spirits (SPIR-uts)
Also known as ghosts. In some
ballets, a person's spirit appears
after he or she has died.

FURTHER READING

Hackett, Jane. *Ballet: A Step-by-Step Guide to the Secrets of Ballet*. How To. New York: DK Publishers, 2011.

Lee, Laura. *A Child's Introduction to Ballet: The Stories, Music, and Magic of Classical Dance*. New York: Black Dog & Leventhal Publishers, 2007.

Mellow, Mary Kate, and Stephanie Troeller. *Prima Princessa's Ballet for Beginners: Featuring the School of American Ballet*. Morganville, NJ: Imagine Publishing, 2010.

Schorer, Suki. *Put Your Best Foot Forward: A Young Dancer's Guide to Life*. New York: Workman Publishing Company, 2005.

WEBSITES

For web resources related to the subject of this book, go to: www.windmillbooks.com/weblinks and select this book's title.

31

INDEX